Jackie Chan

Julia Holt

Published in association with The Basic Skills Agency

Hodder & Stoughton
A MEMBER OF THE HODDER HEADLINE GRO

Acknowledgements
Cover: Rex Features

Photos: p. 2 © Hulton-Deutsch Collection/CORBIS; p. 12 © Bettmann/CORBIS; p. 20 © Tom Day/BFI; p. 22 © Albert Ferreira/Rex Features; p. 25 © David Buchan/Rex Features; p. 27 © Eric Robert/CORBIS.

Orders; please contact Bookpoint Ltd, 130 Milton Park, Abingdon, Oxon OX14 4SB. Telephone (44) 01235 827720, Fax: (44) 01235 400454. Lines are open from 9.00–6.00, Monday to Saturday, with a 24 hour message answering service. You can also order through our website www.hodderheadline.co.uk

British Library Cataloguing in Publication Data
A catalogue record for this title is available from the British Library

ISBN 0 340 87655 7

First published 2003
Impression number   10 9 8 7 6 5 4 3 2 1
Year   2007 2206 2005 2004 2003

Typeset by SX Composing DTP, Rayleigh, Essex.
Printed in Great Britain for Hodder & Stoughton Educational, a division of Hodder Headline, 338 Euston Road, London NW1 3BH by Bath Press Ltd, Bath.

Contents

1 China

Jackie is famous all over the world.
He has made more than 70 films.
But his own story
is more amazing than any of his films.
It involves many countries,
many adventures and many names.

Back in China about 50 years ago,
the Japanese invaded.
Many people had to flee
to keep safe.
Thousands of people
left their families behind.
They tried to get to Hong Kong.
Hong Kong was a safe island
because it was run by Britain.

Two of the people
who made it to Hong Kong,
were a man called Charles
and a woman called Lee Lee.

A lot of Chinese refugees lived in this area of Hong Kong around 1949.

They got married as soon as they landed.
They were very lucky to find work.
Charles became the cook
for the French ambassador in Hong Kong.
Lee Lee became his housekeeper.

Soon after they had a baby boy.
They named him Chan Hong-san.
This means 'born in Hong Kong Chan'.
He was such a big baby
that his nick-name was cannon ball.

When he was born
the hospital bill was $26.
Charles and Lee Lee
didn't have that kind of money.

The doctor offered to adopt the boy
and give them $78.
It was very tempting
for two poor people.

They said "No"
because the baby boy was a symbol
of their new life in Hong Kong.

He was born on 7 April 1954.
This was the year of the horse
which is very lucky in China.
It means that the baby
will have a lot of energy and success.
This turned out to be true
because the baby grew up
to be Jackie Chan.

2 Chan Hong-san

For the first six years
of the little boy's life
the family lived in a big house
with the French ambassador.
They only had one small room
with no window.

Charles was a strict father.
Every morning at dawn
he woke his little boy up.
Together they did push-ups
and lifted bags of sand.
Charles also showed his son
the basics of Kung Fu.

Soon Chan Hong-san
was sent to school.

He messed about,
making the other kids laugh.

The teacher made him stand in the corner
so he learned to fall asleep standing up.
Sadly, this was all he learned at school.
He only went for one year.

In 1961, when the little boy was six,
Charles Chan went to Australia.
He had a new job as head cook
for the American ambassador.

But he could not
take his family with him.

3 The China Drama Academy

Charles did not know what to do
with his six year-old son
In the end the little boy was sent to study
at the China Drama Academy.
It was a circus and theatre school.

He was taken to the academy
in his favourite cowboy outfit.
The master of the academy
said that he would feed him,
give him clothes and teach him.
In return, the master would keep the boy's wages.

Charles told his son:
never join a gang
never take drugs
and never gamble.
Then he went to Australia, to his new job.

The master changed the boy's name
to Yuen Lo.
He went to live at the academy
for ten years, with thirty other kids.
They were all re-named Yuen.

He learned by copying the other kids.
At 5.00am they got up
and ran round the roof-tops five times.
There was rice for breakfast.
Then six hours of
acrobatics and martial arts.
This was followed by soup, rice and fish.
Later the kids could go to the toilet
for the first time that day.

After lunch they practised the splits.
Then they walked on their hands
for half an hour.
Then the academy was cleaned
from top to bottom,
followed by more rice and fish to eat.

After dinner Master Yu went out
and the kids went to lessons.
Sometimes they were badly behaved
until the master came back.

If Master Yu was in a good mood
when he came back,
they learned fun things
like face painting.

They trained for twelve hours a day
between 5.00am – 12.00pm,
followed by five hours of sleep, on the floor.

The only contact
the kids had with the outside world,
was family visits.
Yuen Lo's mum came every week.
She brought sweets,
and big plastic bags full of hot water
to wash his hair.

The rules were strict at the academy.
They did what Master Yu said
or they got the cane.
The newest boy in the academy,
was called Little Brother.
The boy who had been there the longest
was called Biggest Brother.
If the Biggest Brother was a bully
life was hard for the others.

Every now and then
all the kids from the academy
were taken to the theatre.
They went to see the experts
in acrobatics, mime, singing,
stage combat and acting.

Over the next ten years
Yuen Lo's mum came every week.
She always brought hot water.

4　The Stunt Man

Then one day Yuen Lo's mum
left for Australia.
He was adopted by Master Yu.

When Yuen Lo got to the age of twelve
he was chosen to perform
on the stage.
It was a big day for him.
Yuen Lo loved performing.

It meant extra training
but it also meant extra food
and big adventures.

After a time the work changed
Yuen Lo and the other kids
got more and more work in films.

Martial arts films
were becoming popular.
Stunt men were needed.
One by one the drama academies
were closing down.
Yuen Lo made up his mind
to leave his academy
and find work for himself.
It was 1971,
and Yuen Lo was seventeen years old.
To this day there are
many people called Yuen
in martial arts films.
They all come from Master Yu's academy.

Yuen Lo wanted to be a full time stunt man.
Charles Chan bought his son
a flat in Hong Kong.

Now Yuen Lo could start
to build his career.
It was not easy.
Hundreds of boys
from all the academies
were looking for stunt man work.

One day Yuen Lo met Biggest Brother
from the academy.
His name was now Samo Hung
and he was a stunt manager for films.
Samo was working on two new films
with the biggest Chinese star
in the world.
He was called Bruce Lee.
Lots of stunt men were needed.
So Yuen Lo got to work, for $15 a day,
with the famous Bruce Lee.
The films were called
'Fist of Fury' and 'Enter the Dragon'.

The famous actor, Bruce Lee.

5 Jackie Chan

Lots of people
tried to copy Bruce Lee's style.
But when he died very young,
his style of film died with him.
So did the work.
Samo told Yuen Lo
to go to Australia to live with his parents.

That's what he did.
He got an Australian passport.
He even tried to learn English.
Then he got work on a building site.
The men on the site
called him Jackie.
That's how the name
Jackie Chan was born.

Jackie wasn't happy in Australia.
His Mum reminded him
that he was born in the year of the horse.
She told him to try again with films
because he would be successful.

Jackie wrote to everyone he knew
in Hong Kong.
One man wrote back.

He was called Willie Chan.
He was a manager of a film studio.
He wanted Jackie
to come back to Hong Kong
and star in more Bruce Lee style films.
The money was not good,
but Jackie needed to try again.
He went back to Hong Kong.
It was 1976
and he signed an eight year contract.

For the next two years
all Jackie's films were flops.
The Bruce Lee style didn't suit Jackie.
Bruce Lee was serious
and Jackie Chan was funny.

6　Success

Jackie's studio didn't want him any more.
They lent him to another studio.
The new studio took a chance
and made a comedy with him.
It was called
'Snake in the Eagle's Shadow'.
It was a block-buster hit
in Hong Kong.
It made more money
than the Bruce Lee films.

Jackie Chan was a star in Hong Kong.
Kids copied his stunts in the streets.
Newspapers wrote about him.
He started to be paid big money.
He went out and bought
seven diamond watches
in one day.

Other studios wanted Jackie
to work with them.
In 1980, Jackie signed a contract
for $4 million.
Willie Chan became his agent.

After more successful films in Hong Kong,
the studio sent Jackie to the USA
to make a film, in English.
It was 1980.
Jackie was given only two weeks
to learn to speak English.

The film was a flop in the USA.
Jackie's English was not good enough
for the film
or for talking to the media.
He went back home an angry man.

Jackie needed another hit.
So he called Samo Hung
and some other brothers from the academy.
Together they made a successful team.
They made many hit films in Hong Kong
and Jackie developed his trade mark.

Jackie's trade mark
was doing really, really, really
dangerous stunts.
The first one was dropping 50 feet
down a clock tower
to the ground.
The stunt was in a film called
'Project A', in 1983.
It was made in Taiwan.
When he was making the film
Jackie met the top actress in Taiwan.

Her name was Lin Feng-jiao.
Jackie fell in love with her.
He asked her to marry him
and the next weekend
they flew to LA and got married.
The only person at the wedding
was Willie Chan.

The wedding had to be secret
because Jackie's fans
might kill themselves if they knew.
Later, when the fans found out,
one girl did kill herself.

A year after the wedding
their son Jackson was born.

7 Jackie's Films

Jackie Chan's films
are different from American action films.
First, he's always the one
who gets beaten up.
Second, you can tell his stunts are *real*.

He has:
hung from an umbrella from the outside
of a moving bus,
rolled down a mountain
inside a ball,
fallen through five stories of glass
inside a shopping centre,
jumped from a roof
onto a ladder hanging
from a helicopter,
jumped from a cliff
onto the top of a hot air balloon.

Jackie jumping from a moving train in *Shanghai Noon*.

At the end of each film
Jackie shows the mistakes he makes
during the film.
These are always very funny.

Sometimes the mistakes are serious
and he ends up in hospital.
Once he had to have brain surgery
when he fell out of a tree.
The surgery was a success
but he has a hole
in his skull to this day.

Jackie has broken
almost every bone in his body.
He's even been slashed by a sword
that should have been blunt
but he always comes back for more.

Jackie Chan with Jean Claude Van Damme at the opening of
Planet Hollywood in Singapore.

8 The USA

By the 1990s,
Jackie Chan had done almost everything.
He owned houses.
He was a partner in th restaurant chain
Planet Hollywood.
The Queen had given him an MBE.

The only thing he hadn't done
was to be a star in the USA.
Samo Hung had made it with his TV series
'Martial Law'.
So in 1996,
Jackie tried once more.

This time he got the right film.
It was called
'Rumble In The Bronx'.
This time he was much better
at talking to the media.

The film was a big hit in Hong Kong
and a block-buster in The USA.
It made $32 million.

Finally the forty-one year old Jackie Chan
was a star world wide.

It was the first Hong Kong film ever
to be a box office number one
in the USA.
From then on all his films
have been hits in both countries.

'Highbinders' will be his 111th film.
Jackie stars in this film
with the British comic Lee Evans.
Very soon he will start work
on the re-make of
'Around the World In Eighty Days'.
There will also be a Jackie Chan
cartoon show out soon.

Jackie at the premiere of *The Tuxedo* in Los Angeles, 2002.

Jackie is the biggest action film star
in the world.
But how long can he keep doing it?

Will he be a sixty year-old
action hero?
Or will he turn to directing films?

Whatever Jackie does
he will give it 110%.

What does the future hold for Jackie Chan?